3   712.609423 HOW

LEARNING.
·········services

01209 722146

Duchy College Rosewarne
Learning Centre

This resource is to be returned on or before the last date
stamped below. To renew items please contact the Centre

Three Week Loan

RETURNED

D0417047

Heligan Wild

Heligan Wild

A Year of Nature in the Lost Gardens

COLIN HOWLETT

ILLUSTRATED BY MALLY FRANCIS
AND ANGUS HUDSON

INTRODUCTION BY TIM SMIT

Victor Gollancz
London

First published in Great Britain 1999
by Victor Gollancz
An imprint of the Orion Publishing Group Ltd
Wellington House, 125 Strand, London WC2R 0BB

Text © Colin Howlett 1999
Illustrations © Mally Francis and Angus Hudson 1999
Introduction © Tim Smit 1999

The right of Colin Howlett, Mally Francis and Angus Hudson to be
identified as authors of this work has been asserted by them in
accordance with the Copyright, Designs and Patents Act, 1988.

A CIP record for this book is available
from the British Library.

ISBN 0 575 06751 9

Designed and typeset by Production Line, Minster Lovell, Oxford
Printed in Great Britain by Butler and Tanner Ltd, Frome, Somerset

All rights reserved. No part of this publication may be reproduced
or transmitted in any form or by any means, electronic or mechanical
including photocopying, recording or any information storage or
retrieval system, without prior permission in writing from the publishers.

This book is sold subject to the condition that it shall not, by way of trade
or otherwise, be lent, resold, hired out, or otherwise circulated without the
publisher's prior consent in any form of binding or cover other than that
in which it is published and without a similar condition including this
condition being imposed on the subsequent purchaser.

2 4 6 8 9 7 5 3 1

For Sarah –

who, for so many years, has indulged my urge
to roam wild places and who has faithfully
followed my every footstep

map drawn by Ruth Perkins

Contents

Introduction

In the summer of 1975, as an archaeology student, I decided to go on a tour of the major prehistoric sites of the south-west. Candy, my future wife, came along for the ride and together we explored the beautiful Gloucestershire countryside, savouring totally separate experiences. Most of the ancient monuments I wanted to seek out were well off the beaten track, set in some of the finest scenery that Britain has to offer. Although they were designated heritage sites they remained largely undisturbed by visitors, save for intrepid romantics like me, whose idea of a good time was to crawl on my hands and knees into the depths of those incredible tombs, imagining myself back in time. I remember emerging from Hetty Pegler's Tump to find Candy completely unmoved by the object of my excitement, for she was enraptured by the wildflowers that seemed to prosper so well around the same area.

So began my painful rote learning of the names of native flora: 'pink' campion; purple loosestrife and the infamous rosebay willowherb (which I could never tell apart); herb

Rosebay willowherb

robert, which I always remembered because it sounded like a sax player, toadflax, for the same reason; and dozens more whose names resolutely refused to stick. There are none so blind as those that will not see. Now I smile at the man I was and marvel at how I've changed.

Some years later, after we moved to Cornwall, my archaeological interest was stirred again when by chance I came upon the wilderness that was the Lost Gardens of Heligan. I fell in love with the place and, together with my friend John Nelson, set about restoring it to the form and function it had enjoyed in its heyday. Now, nearly one hundred acres of pleasure grounds and productive gardens are vibrant once more, bustling with activity and laden with produce.

Throughout the restoration Heligan drew people to it like a magnet. Some volunteered for a short time, while others chose to stay on and stake their futures with us. The common attribute of them all was their versatility. Colin Howlett was one such person. On taking early retirement he had moved to Gorran Haven, where I met him in our local pub, the Llawnroc, in 1993. Here, over a beer, he would often talk of his passion for wildlife. One thing led to another, and within a year Colin had become our marketing director, health and safety officer and, by accident, our weatherman. He undertook every task with a meticulous attention to detail and unquestionable commitment. His interest in natural history has found an echo among the rest of the team, and as we ponder the next phase of the restoration – our move from the gardens into the wider estate – the issue of protecting and nurturing the biodiversity found here has become the overriding concern.

Colin's delightful, intimate journal of the observations he made throughout 1995 has become symbolic of the reawakening of the wider estate. If it was chance that Colin became the weatherman, then it was the purest serendipity that not just one, but two talented illustrators should be found among the residents and staff at Heligan. The exquisite water-colours of flora by Mally Francis and fauna by Angus Hudson bring this lovely volume to life and are a testament to the breadth of talent within the team. I am proud to introduce you to Heligan Wild.

Tim Smit
January 1999

Foreword

In the very early days of the Heligan restoration project, individuals joining the team did so without having the remotest idea of what they were letting themselves in for. For most of us, the jobs we thought we were taking on bore no relationship whatsoever to the tasks we eventually found ourselves performing. They were heady days, full of the excitement of new discoveries.

I personally arrived at Heligan in March 1993, having been introduced to the project director, Tim Smit, by my friend John Nelson (Tim's colleague). It was proposed that I should join the team to assist with the sale of tickets in the newly opened ticket office. Within weeks, Tim had adjusted that role to include the management of all marketing functions, personnel manager, health and safety officer, photographer, sweeper and raker of the reception area, sometime toilet-cleaning wallah, digger of kitchen gardens, lecturer, tour guide, identifier and labeller of native tree species and resident weather observer.

Tim had been approached by the Meteorological Office in Bracknell about establishing an official weather station on the Heligan estate. 'That's a great idea,' said Tim, and promptly 'volunteered' me to run it! Thus, in one fell swoop he had condemned me to an early morning hike (365 days a year and in all weather conditions) to record the many readings required by Bracknell. The Weather Station was eventually sited on the East Lawn (now a meadow, but formerly part of the extensive lawns of Heligan House), approximately three-quarters of a mile from the entrance to the Heligan estate.

Throughout my life I have been fascinated by all things wild. My early morning walks to the Weather Station proved to be the ideal opportunity for me to indulge my love of nature and I was soon recording every detail of the flora and fauna observed during those walks. One of my other responsibilities, that of health and safety co-ordinator on site, called for the daily inspection of the many miles of paths open to the public. This duty was therefore combined with that of weather observer, and each day I varied my route to and from the Weather Station.

The diary that follows was compiled from notes taken throughout 1995, and subsequently illustrated by my two friends, Mally Francis and Angus Hudson, both of whom are closely connected to Heligan and share my love of wildlife. We hope that readers will experience just a little of the immense pleasure that we have gained from observing the changing seasons within this wild and beautiful place. Welcome to Heligan.

Colin Howlett
January 1999

Weekly Observations

1 January

Hail showers early today and a sharp ground frost overnight. Four degrees of frost at ground level in the Weather Station, but bright periods between the showers give promise of a pleasant day. A mistle thrush sings his territorial song from the topmost branches of a large beech in the Northern Gardens. Robins also exchange song from different parts of the garden, each bird establishing its own territory well in advance of the breeding season.

8 January

Overcast, mild and damp today. Snowdrops flowering in the Jungle garden and cock pheasants displaying on the grass by the Weather Station. Several goldcrests sighted on the Woodland Walk. They appear totally fearless, coming to within a few feet of me, their high pitched communication calls piping out from trees and shrubs on both sides of the walk.

15 January

Overcast, dull and mild. Dry, with light winds. The mistle thrush continues his territorial song in the Northern Gardens and a nuthatch catches my eye as it runs up the trunk of an oak tree along the Woodland Walk. First signs of ramsons (garlic) and bluebells thrusting through the leaf litter in the Jungle and many primroses now blooming. A small flock of long-tailed tits is spotted in the treetops along the Woodland Walk, each bird keeping in touch with others in the group by the continuous use of its communication call.

22 January

Raining today, but mild with light winds. A kestrel on the fence by the Northern Summerhouse takes a long, hard look at me before flying off. Coal tits in the tree rhododendrons by the Grotto and again seen on the Woodland Walk. Wrens, dunnocks, chaffinches all active and there is much birdsong. Rosettes of foxglove leaves appearing all over the wildest parts of the gardens.

Snowdrop   *Goldcrests*

Mistle thrush

Long-tailed tits

29 January

Overcast with strong gusty winds from the west, but mild with drizzle in the wind. A grey day. Surprised to see a peregrine falcon circling, sickle-shaped, approximately a hundred feet above the dovecote. Then with rapid wingbeats it turns swiftly towards the east and disappears from view. The doves seem oblivious to the danger that certainly threatened them until my arrival on the scene. A pair of bullfinches sighted in the brambles close to the Weather Station. This is the third sighting within a few days so they may be setting up territory. The cock bird, with his bright salmon chest and white rump, is in superb condition.

5 February

Foggy, 'Cornish mist' and very mild with everything dripping. A mosses and lichens day. Too foggy to see much in the Jungle but birdsong all around. First celandines flowering in the grass in the Weather Station compound and also along the Woodland Walk. Campion seedlings appearing in large clumps all over the Jungle. Along the Woodland Walk, goldcrests flit through the honeysuckle in their search for the few insects available to them at this time of year. Incessant high-pitched contact calls keep these tiny birds in touch with each other while they forage in the dense woodland undergrowth.

Primrose   *Celandine and Pennywort*

Nuthatches

Coal tits   Chaffinch

26 February

Bright and clear today with the wind in the north-west and large cumulus clouds sailing over Heligan. Hailstones lying in small drifts on the East Lawn give evidence of a heavy shower that passed close to dawn. With the exception of a song thrush high in the sycamores on the east slope of the Jungle, birdsong is somewhat subdued, probably as a result of the nip in the wind. Hazel catkins on the fringes of the wood are now mature and pollinating and look marvellous with the early morning sun on them. First signs of sycamore buds bursting on low level branches within the Woodland Walk. It is good to see a pair of stock doves in the big lime tree near the entrance to the Jungle. This is the second time in recent days that I have startled them as I pass.

Sycamore buds   *Common dog violet*

CORNWALL COLLEGE
LRC

4 March

Bright and clear today but overnight snow has left a thin powdery covering. Rabbit tracks run in all directions around the Weather Station and these are criss-crossed with the prints of birds, large and small. Stock doves in the lime tree again – must be setting up home there.

Ramsons   *Golden saxifrage*

5 March

A blustery day that promises heavy showers and gales later. Overcast and damp but milder than of late. My arrival on the East Lawn is greeted by the alarm calls of jay, magpie and cock pheasant. As I leave the Weather Station two resident buzzards flap furiously for height to challenge a third bird circling high against the leaden sky. No thermals today, so gaining altitude means hard work for such large birds. The birdsong in the Jungle is once again all around me. For several days the hail, sleet and snowstorms have resulted in an almost silent Jungle garden. As I leave the woodland a small flock of redwings rises from the lawn in front of the Big House and perches silently in the sycamores to watch me pass by. These Scandinavian thrushes will soon depart on their homeward migration.

12 March

A beautiful, crisp, clear morning with virtually no wind. Birdsong all around as I enter the East Lawn and I hear the intermittent drumming of a woodpecker on hollow wood. The first violet flowers of the wild periwinkle have appeared on the Woodland Walk and not twenty-five yards from the tearoom a doe rabbit hops across the path right in front of me, carrying a bundle of moss and dried grass

Dunnock

in her jaws. She disappears beneath a fallen tree root. No doubt she will bear her young within the week. In the Ravine I catch the unmistakable twin notes of the tiny chiffchaff. Singing from his perch high in the lucombe oak, he is the first to be heard this spring and has probably only just arrived here after his epic migration flight, possibly from as far afield as Africa. The first flowers of ramsons and wood violets are appearing in the Jungle and the scent of garlic is heavy on the air.

19 March

Blustery showers and bright periods will be the order for today. Trees in the Woodland Walk are swaying and bending but in the Jungle all is calm as the strong winds pass overhead, deflected by both the contours of the land and the shelter belt around the gardens. There is virtually no disturbance at ground level. Bird activity is now intense and everywhere I hear the songs of thrushes, robins, dunnocks, wrens, chiffchaffs and chaffinches. High in the giant conifers a small flock of goldcrests is active, each tiny bird calling to the others with its high-pitched single note. This, the smallest of the British birds, appears totally fearless of man but, with its preference for the uppermost branches of large conifer trees, it is more often heard than seen.

Wrens

26 March

Several fine, mild days have resulted in an acceleration of growth in ground-level plants all over the Jungle. Patches of primroses are everywhere, together with the starry white spikes of ramsons. The song thrush sings from his usual perch, high in the topmost branches of a sycamore tree, and another thrush responds from a neighbouring territory at the head of the Jungle. As I go down the boardwalk towards the lowest pond a pair of jays follows my progress from a safe distance, flitting silently from treetop to treetop. In the Woodland Walk a single coal tit hunts insects among the fresh young leaves in the lower branches of a sycamore. While I watch, I am surprised to see it joined by a pair of long-tailed tits.

2 April

Today dawns grey with a light drizzle in the air, but mild and virtually calm. Birds are active everywhere: singing, collecting nesting material and feeding first broods of chicks. I watch a robin, her beak full of food, fly to her nest hidden behind the peeling bark of a dead treetrunk and I resist the urge to take a closer look. A female blackbird gathers nesting material among the leaf litter by the board-walk and a blue tit disappears into a tiny hole high in a bare treetrunk. The first bluebells are now appearing in the Jungle together with white wood sorrel and all around are patches of lime-coloured golden saxifrage.

Song thrush

9 April

The weather has been dry and warm for several days and growth of woodland plants in the Jungle is now advancing apace with hardly an inch of bare soil to be seen anywhere. Every woodpigeon and collared dove for miles around seems to be calling from the treetops and other bird activity is equally intense.

16 April

The dry spell continues and the Jungle is a riot of colour with wild flowers everywhere: within a few yards, wild bugle, yellow pimpernel, ramsons, golden saxifrage, herb

Wild bugle

robert, ground ivy, bluebells, common dog violets, wood sorrel and primroses. All around, birds are busily going about their affairs, searching for food and nesting material. Greenfinches, goldfinches, blue tits, great tits, coal tits and long-tailed tits are all spotted within minutes of entering the woodland.

23 April

Today is a marked improvement upon yesterday's torrential rain and low temperatures. Red campion has joined the numerous other wild flowers now blooming on the woodland floor, and broadleaved trees all over the estate are bursting with fresh new growth. Throughout the woodland different tree species can be identified by the many and varied shades of pale green that each displays in its new leaves.

30 April

The day starts overcast, mild and with just a gentle breeze to stir the higher branches of the trees in the Jungle. As I quietly make my way down the east side of the valley two herons, startled by my sudden appearance, flap desperately to get airborne from the third pond. They climb steeply out through the treetops on their huge and powerful wings.

Wood sorrel

As this pond has not yet
been stocked with fish, it
is likely that they have
discovered the eels and
frogs that live there.
The display of
wild flowers
throughout the
wooded areas is
now at its best and visitors to the
garden are being treated to a blaze of
colour. The first sightings this year of
speckled wood butterflies: two males, typically
circling each other in a shaft of sunlight that
pierces the woodland canopy. Each one will
compete for his own territory, a woodland glade,
in which to waylay passing females.

Chiffchaff   *Yellow pimpernel*

7 May

For the eighth day in succession, the dawn comes with a clear blue sky and just a hint of a breeze to stir the woodland trees. Another glorious day in prospect. All over the woodland floor ferns are uncurling their fronds in response to the longer, warmer days of late spring. They will push aside any other plants that impede them as they stretch to gather as much light as possible beneath the woodland canopy. The sycamores are in full leaf now, lime green at this time of year but destined to turn a deeper shade as the year progresses. Among their leaves the flowers hang like miniature bunches of grapes, laden with pollen

and already commanding the attention of numerous buzzing insects. The tall stems of foxgloves are forming flower buds now and are so numerous this year that we can expect a wonderful show of colour from them very shortly. These will replace the bluebells and other, earlier wild flowers as their blooms slowly fade.

14 May

Cold and clear today, with temperatures dropping overnight to minus 4.7 degrees Celsius. The laughing call of the green woodpecker greets my entry into the Jungle although as usual he is careful not to show himself. The bluebells and ramsons on the woodland floor are now fading, and the red campion is in full flower. These will shortly be superseded by numerous foxgloves, rosebay willowherb and figwort, all of which have now grown to their full height and have formed their flower buds. A few plants of common twayblade have been spotted by one of our senior gardeners and I check to see if they are in flower. Not yet, but their flower spikes are well formed and a few days should do the trick. As I walk up past the front of the Big House a pair of goldfinches flit from sapling to sapling a few yards ahead of me, twittering as they go, and swifts, swallows and house martins wheel overhead. Along the Woodland Walk I spot several flowers of the cuckoo-pint pushing up through the thick leaf litter, and where only last week there were tightly curled fronds of bracken and other ferns, today the plants are spreading to cover every inch of the woodland.

Bluebells

Jay   *Red campion*

20 May

Several days of quiet, warm and sunny weather have turned the woodland floor of the Jungle into a lush and dense carpet of wild plants. The first spikes of foxgloves are now flowering side by side with campion, buttercups and drifts of speedwell. I am delighted to see a pair of mallard on the second pond. Resting motionless on a part-sunken branch that overhangs the water, they appear unconcerned at my presence. Both birds are in superb condition with the drake displaying his iridescent blues and greens in the early sunlight. A few yards further along the path a flash of white and salmon betrays a pair of bullfinches as they fly up the valley. On the Woodland Walk I am surrounded by a whole family of goldcrests scattered among the lower branches of a sycamore tree, the young all clamouring to be fed as the parent birds flit frantically from leaf to leaf gathering aphids. I am always amazed at the lack of fear these tiny birds show, apparently too busy even to notice me standing a few feet beneath them.

28 May

The skies above Heligan are overcast with low, scudding clouds giving occasional spells of light rain. Heavier showers are forecast for later. As I approach the Weather Station a single buzzard flies low over the East Lawn and, on sighting me, climbs swiftly and effortlessly in the wind gradient above the Jungle, converting his speed into height.

Speedwell

Herons   *Cuckoo-pint*

A quick check on the few plants of common twayblade recently spotted on the woodland floor is rewarded with just a few flower spikes of these undramatic but interesting members of the orchid family. The pair of mallard, first spotted last week on the second pond, are today feeding contentedly on Top Lake and may well remain with us now to raise a family.

4 June

Overnight rain and now large cumulus clouds are forming over Heligan, threatening further heavy showers for later this morning. Early morning bird activity in the Jungle is close to frenetic with birdsong emanating from every direction and family groups of various tits all clamouring to be fed. Only the drake mallard is seen on the second pond today. It is quite possible that his mate is now sitting on a clutch of eggs, probably among the dense bamboo beside the pond. A spotted flycatcher repeatedly swoops out of the lower branches of the giant redwood to seize flying insects, then returns to her vantage point overlooking the valley. She is almost certainly nesting in one of the deep fissures that naturally occur in the soft bark of the redwood's massive trunk. Recent wet, humid weather has brought a dense lushness to the valley floor and a tremendous increase in insect activity. This is a time of plenty for the woodland birds, and food is abundant for the many now busy raising families.

Green woodpecker

Twayblade

12 June

Bright and clear today but cool with light winds from the north-east. As I approach the Weather Station, several baby rabbits are grazing the short grass around the beehives. Immediately they bolt for cover among the surrounding brambles. On the walk across the East Lawn towards the Jungle I disturb a common blue butterfly which flies just a few feet to the nearest patch of horseshoe vetch and settles, wings closed, to await the first warming rays of the sun. Throughout the wooded areas huge numbers of foxgloves are now blooming, with drifts of purple flower spikes scattered among the other woodland plants. The constant drone of bumble-bees can be heard as they busily visit flower after flower. Lower down the Jungle, close to the bottom pond, my attention is drawn to insect activity on the gravel bed by the stream. Hundreds of honey bees are flying in to land on the gravel, pausing only briefly to drink and then flying off again. I watch, fascinated, for several minutes as a steady stream of bees arrives and departs.

18 June

A thin overcast masks the sun today and with virtually no breeze at ground level the air in the Jungle feels heavy and damp. Birdsong throughout the valley is as mixed as usual with woodpigeons, collared doves, jays, magpies, jackdaws and a host of smaller birds competing for attention. As I stand on the boardwalk close to the third pond a blackcap

Herb robert   Foxgloves

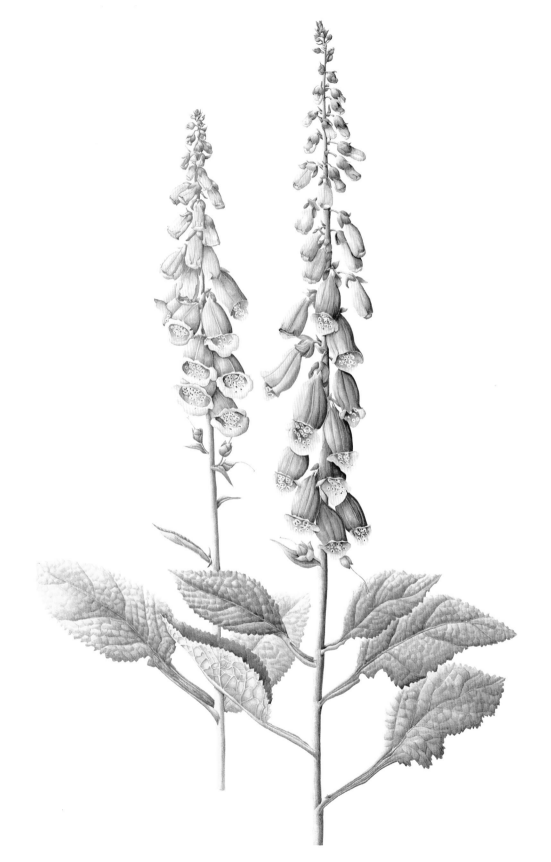

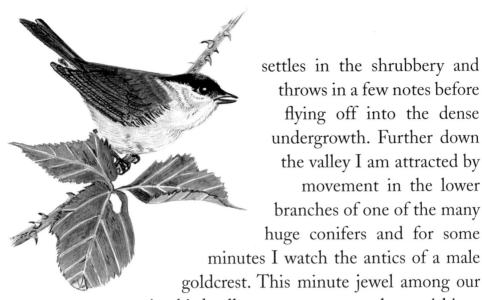

settles in the shrubbery and throws in a few notes before flying off into the dense undergrowth. Further down the valley I am attracted by movement in the lower branches of one of the many huge conifers and for some minutes I watch the antics of a male goldcrest. This minute jewel among our native birds allows me to approach to within a few feet, as he busies himself with the task of searching for aphids in the fir needles. In the topmost branches of the same tree several other goldcrests can be heard as they flit from twig to twig high up in the canopy.

25 June

Just a thin layer of low cloud covers the sun this morning, but all the signs are that this will burn off later giving yet another beautiful, sunny day. As I leave the Weather Station and turn towards the Jungle valley, the first meadow brown butterflies are already on the wing among the long grasses of the East Lawn. In the Jungle I pause on the bridge by the second pond and watch a family of marsh tits as they hunt for insects in the huge honeysuckle that climbs some forty feet into an oak tree beside the path. As I watch, a sudden movement on the water's surface attracts my attention and I am just in time to see a tiny water

Blackcap   Swallow

shrew emerge. It swims swiftly through the pondside vegetation, climbs on to the muddy bank, pauses only briefly and then runs back to the water's edge to plunge beneath the surface again. Just a glimpse of one of our smallest and most interesting mammals. Further down the valley, along the marshy fringes of the stream, the tall flower spikes of valerian and chervil have joined the foxgloves, and insect activity among the many flowers is frenetic.

2 July

Warm and very humid this morning with a thin overcast veiling the sun. It is now fifteen days since our last rain and no sign of a break in the long, dry spell. As I walk through the Northern Gardens I am greeted by a small but angry swarm of large bumble-bees whose underground nest at the base of the Mount has been unceremoniously dug up overnight by a badger. Soil and stones scatter the path and a big cavity about one foot across and equally deep is all that remains of what had been their home. Badgers just love bumble-bee grubs and honey! On the East Lawn large numbers of meadow brown and skipper butterflies are on the wing and a huge blue-bodied dragonfly hunts insects over the long grass. In the Jungle the resident birds take little notice of my passing, and chiffchaff, spotted flycatcher, great spotted woodpecker and an unidentified warbler are all sighted as I stand quietly leaning on the

Great spotted woodpecker

bridge by the second pond. Groups of whirligig beetles circle each other in a seemingly endless dance on the glassy surface of the pool, while pond skaters and water boatmen are to be seen in large numbers as they hunt for prey.

9 July

Clear blue skies herald yet another beautiful summer's day. It is now twenty-two days since any rain fell at Heligan, and everything looks parched and dry. The barley in the meadow alongside the new orchard is ripening fast and will no doubt be harvested shortly. Halfway to the Jungle, I am entertained by five long-tailed tits performing antics in the large, solitary sycamore that overhangs the path. A jackdaw emerges from a hollow and immediately squawks its alarm call. On the boundaries of the East Lawn large numbers of butterflies are taking advantage of the warm sunshine. Attracted by the profusion of bramble flowers, peacocks, gatekeepers, meadow browns, ringlets and green-veined whites are all active and many skippers are seen flitting among the seeding grasses. Low over Old Wood a single buzzard soars on rigid, outstretched wings, slowly circling in an invisible thermal of rising air. Throughout the Jungle and all along the Woodland Walk the dainty white flowers of enchanter's nightshade are now in bloom, while towering above them the foxgloves have turned their attention to setting seed. High summer has arrived.

Enchanter's nightshade

16 July

A few showers yesterday and during the night have broken the long dry spell and the air is warm and humid. We can expect further thundery showers later today. As I walk down to the Weather Station small flocks of greenfinches, chaffinches and goldfinches move ahead of me, each family group sticking closely to its own kind and each emitting its own distinctive communication call. Arriving on the East Lawn I spend a few moments watching a magnificent peacock butterfly that has settled at eye level on a bramble flower not a foot from me. Newly emerged from its chrysalis it is in superb condition, too busy feeding on nectar to notice me. The Jungle is, as usual, full of early morning bird activity and I am delighted to watch yet another pair of goldcrests frantically feeding their four newly fledged youngsters among the lower branches of a huge conifer. Higher up the valley, close to Top Lake, a pair of bullfinches allow me to get within a few feet of where they are busily enjoying a meal of figwort buds. It is the first time I have seen them feeding on this plant. Top Lake is again alive with movement as numerous pond insects scurry across the surface, while low over the water a single blue dragonfly hunts its prey.

23 July

A beautiful morning with clear blue skies and virtually no wind. As I approach the Weather Station a huge brown cockchafer beetle buzzes past my head, crash-lands on the

Peacock butterfly   Red admiral butterfly

Bullfinches

Emperor dragonfly

Greenfinches

path just ahead of me and begins to burrow into the loose turf, where it quickly disappears from sight. My entry into the Jungle is greeted by the alarm call of a great spotted woodpecker and on this occasion I am lucky enough to get a really good view of this beautifully marked little bird as it marches up and down the vertical trunk of a large oak tree. As I continue down the Jungle boardwalk towards the third pond, its larger relative, the green woodpecker, also makes an appearance, swooping down from a sycamore. With its typical dipping flight, it quickly disappears into the dense woodland beyond the Jungle. A few minutes later, as I start to walk back from the Jungle, my attention is caught by the buzzing of thousands of bees, wasps, hoverflies and numerous other flying insects as they feed on the flowers of the huge lime tree. The tree is literally alive with activity and when I reach the top of the hill the drone of insect wings can still be heard.

30 July

Following a night of heavy thunderstorms the sky is leaden and, with not even the slightest breeze to stir the trees, the air is heavy, warm and humid. As I walk down the rough track leading to the East Lawn the total stillness is suddenly broken by the rhythmic drumming of a great spotted woodpecker as it hammers on a dead bough among

Figwort

the upper branches of a large beech tree. I am showered by small pieces of rotten wood, and judging from the amount of chippings on the path, he's been excavating for several days. Within the Weather Station compound, grasshoppers jump in all directions. As I stoop to read and reset the ground thermometers, their rasping song is all around me, emanating from the long grasses of the East Lawn. Several species of butterflies are on the wing; painted lady, red admiral, peacock, meadow brown and gatekeeper are all within view. Even though it is early morning and there is no sun to warm them, the lack of wind and the high humidity have enabled them to become active.

6 August

Overnight rain has left everywhere dripping and refreshed, and the morning dawns calm with just a thin overcast to veil the sun. On my walk down to the Weather Station the shrill cry of a young buzzard echoes across the valley and just a few minutes later I catch sight of an adult bird flying low over the Jungle canopy. Even as I watch this huge bird

Blackberry

(the largest of our native hawks), a small family group of goldcrests (our smallest native bird) can be clearly heard among the topmost branches of a huge conifer. At several places along the Woodland Walk I get fleeting glimpses of warblers as they dart for cover in the dense undergrowth on either side of the path. They are silent today, and without the benefit of song it is virtually impossible to identify which species I am seeing.

13 August

Following overnight showers the skies are now clear, the air is crisp and it is much less humid than of late. As I make my way down the path by the Big House, no fewer than five spotted flycatchers flit from post to post ahead of me, almost certainly a newly fledged family group. Behind the Weather Station, the field that many years ago was the East Lawn of the Big House has now been cut and the smell of new-mown hay is heavy on the still morning air. In the future this area will be managed as a wild flower meadow, capable of supporting a wide range of plant species, butterflies and other insects. All the bird species I have become accustomed to seeing regularly in the Jungle are actively going about their business. I pause in the usual spots to watch and listen. While I am standing on the boardwalk immediately below Top Lake, a sudden splash close to the far bank attracts my attention. There, rising from the disturbed surface of the water, I see the electric blue flash of plumage that can only be that of a kingfisher. For a few seconds the bird perches on the boardwalk and then proceeds to beat some unhappy prey senseless against the timber, before swallowing it and streaking away through the dense shrubbery.

Kingfisher

Grey wagtails

Honeysuckle   *Speckled wood butterflies*

This is the first sighting of this lovely bird since the ponds in the Jungle have been restored, and with any luck it will now become a regular visitor to Heligan.

20 August

Yet another clear, hot day in prospect with only the slightest of breezes. The grass around the Weather Station is parched and burned brown by the many days of hot, dry weather we have had, but the brambles along the perimeter of the woodland appear none the worse for the drought and are covered with ripening blackberries. Close to Top Lake in the Jungle a chiffchaff suddenly starts up with its monotonous two-note song, this after several weeks of silence while it raised its family. The pond is a hive of activity with dragonflies and damselflies darting low over the water as they hunt insects on the wing, and two male speckled wood butterflies circle each other in a shaft of sunlight. On the far bank a pair of grey wagtails are also hunting for insects along the muddy shoreline. These beautiful birds with their yellow and grey plumage are not normally seen here except during their migration, and their arrival indicates that some birds are already moving south.

House martin

27 August

The morning has dawned fine but a good deal cooler than of late. As I walk down to the Weather Station on the east side of the Big House the usual group of greenfinches flies up from where they are feeding among the chamomile plants, beneath the apple trees in the new orchard. Further on, a small flock of a dozen or so spotted flycatchers, together with several warblers, flits from post to post along the fence ahead of me. Within a few days these birds will have left Heligan to begin their journey south to where they will overwinter, possibly as far away as Africa. Just before I enter the trees at the lower end of the walk, a buzzard launches itself from a fence post and glides down the slope and out over the neighbouring fields. Another buzzard circling high overhead repeatedly gives out its mewing call and then descends steeply to sweep out of sight over Old Wood. Today just one grey wagtail is spotted strutting up and down the fallen treetrunk that lies across the third pond in the Jungle. It takes alarm at my presence and flies off down the valley. All around is the now familiar sound of the resident goldcrests as they constantly call each other from the dense shrubbery on either side of the path. Standing motionless beside the pond, I am nevertheless spotted by an ever-watchful jay and within seconds the peace of the whole valley is shattered as his raucous cry spreads through the treetops. Immediately, the woodland is strangely silent and still, but within a few seconds the natural background noises and movements resume and all is normal again.

CORNWALL COLLEGE
LRC

Heavy overnight rain has at last broken the long period of drought, and for the first time in many weeks the rain gauge in the Weather Station proudly announces 11.5 mm of rainfall in the previous twenty-four hours. While I am recording the weather readings a flock of twelve magpies and one jay fly in line astern out of the topmost branches of a large oak on the boundary of the East Lawn. The magpies all disappear, one by one, into the Jungle and the lone jay peels off and departs stage left into Old Wood. On the gate of the Weather Station a red admiral butterfly sits wide-winged and motionless as it absorbs the first warming rays of the sun and only reluctantly takes flight as I leave the compound. Long before I reach the Jungle the sound of

assorted birdsong drifts up from the wooded valley to greet me and, once I am among the trees, the dripping vegetation gives evidence of the heavy overnight rain. The pair of grey wagtails are again spotted flitting between the three largest ponds. Unlike pied wagtails, they appear nervous of humans and as I arrive beside one pond they immediately move on to another further up the valley. The twelve magpies are now squabbling noisily among the bare branches in the crown of the huge, dead Monterey pine that stands sentinel above the west slope of the Jungle. Their antics are too much for a peaceful pair of stock doves roosting lower down and they quickly fly off to find tranquillity elsewhere. At the head of the valley, where the lawn in front of the Big House sweeps down to meet Top Lake, I pause to watch two carrion crows as they strut back and forth in their search for food. No doubt the overnight rain has softened the turf and made a hunt for earthworms a worthwhile proposition.

Chamomile *Hazel nuts*

10 September

Dark, lowering skies today, and after heavy overnight rain it is still pouring down as I enter the Weather Station. In the Jungle the water level in the ponds is at last showing signs of rising again and will soon be back to normal. On Top Lake an enormous raft of whirligig beetles (I estimate well over a thousand) is spinning around on the rain-puckered surface. The numbers of these little beetles appear to have increased steadily over the past few weeks. In the rhododendrons above the pool a single chiffchaff is calling and this, together with one grey wagtail, is the only bird prepared to be seen or heard on such a dismal day.

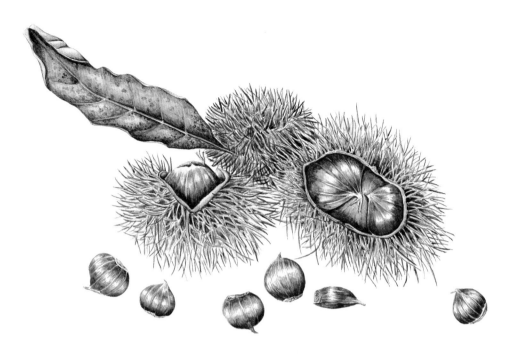

17 September

Breezy this morning with cumulus clouds forming early. Birdsong in the Jungle is now less varied, many of the species having started their migration south. Wrens, robins, goldcrests, chiffchaffs and dunnocks are still voicing their presence, but blackcaps, spotted flycatchers and willow warblers have already left for warmer climes and the skies above the valley are no longer full of wheeling house martins, swallows or swifts. Very shortly the chiffchaff will also leave us. The first signs of autumn are now apparent as the fruits and berries ripen on many shrubs and trees. Beside the second pond the honeysuckle vine that climbs some thirty feet into the large oak is adorned with glossy

Wild rose hips   *Sweet chestnuts*

Magpies   Blackbirds

scarlet berries, and the hips of wild rose are to be seen at various places throughout the woodland. At the top end of the Jungle the leaves on the huge lime tree are now changing to various shades of yellow, and many other woodland trees are also showing their first autumnal colour.

24 September

Heavy overnight rain has left everything dripping, and overhead small cumulus clouds are scudding past on the strong, blustery wind. A large flock of rooks rises into the turbulent air above the stubble field in front of the Stewardry and circles noisily over the ruins of the old kennels. Just a few yards further and five mistle thrushes leave, line astern, from the topmost branches of the large sycamore, each bird rasping out its alarm call as it flies towards the huge Monterey pines that surround the Northern Gardens. As is often the case in strong wind conditions, the Jungle valley is almost devoid of birdsong and I glimpse only the occasional wren and robin in the undergrowth. Close to the third pond I surprise a grey squirrel; caught in the open on the valley floor, it scampers for the safety of the treetops. As I progress slowly along the boardwalk I spot several more squirrels all busily hunting for nuts and seeds among the leaf litter. Sweet chestnuts, beechmast, acorns and hazelnuts are abundant in the surrounding woodland.

1 October

Clear skies over Heligan today with a real autumnal nip in the air. As I walk alongside the shelter belt on the eastern edge of the Northern Gardens, flocks of jackdaws and rooks rise from the stubble in the neighbouring meadow and cackle and caw from the tops of the mature trees along the boundary. From the East Lawn I watch another group of rooks wheeling and tumbling high above the Jungle canopy. Four of these birds break away from the main flock to dive on a single kestrel circling beneath them and with much clamour they drive the offending falcon away down the valley. The Jungle now has the distinctive smell of autumn and all over the woodland floor the many and various fruiting bodies of fungi are

Cuckoo-pint berries *Lime leaf*

springing up through the leaf litter or sprouting from rotting timber. The sheer variety of form and colour in the fungi to be seen at this time of year is staggering.

8 October

A truly beautiful morning, with cloudless skies, just the gentlest of breezes and every leaf glistening with droplets of dew. Among the clumps of long grass on the East Lawn, a myriad cobwebs sparkle like rainbow-coloured necklaces, evidence of the remarkable numbers of spiders that make this meadow their home. As is always the case in calm weather, the Jungle woodland appears alive with bird life even though some species have now departed for their winter quarters. Just beyond the third pond the large conifers are full of assorted members of the tit family. Long-tailed tits, great tits, blue tits and coal tits all dart among the branches, chattering as they go. Further down, near the

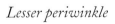

Lesser periwinkle

bottom pond, a single grey wagtail chases flies on the gravel shallows that feed into the last pool. On the gentle climb back up the far side of the valley, the large rotting log that lies beside the boardwalk is now smothered end to end with brown honey fungus. When I arrive at Top Lake the grey wagtail is patrolling the mud beneath the boardwalk. For some minutes I take a really close look at this bird through my binoculars, admiring its grey back, pale belly and primrose yellow rump.

15 October

Overcast and mild again today with just the gentlest of breezes to stir the treetops. Looking across from the Weather Station towards the Jungle, the sky above is a hive of activity with a large, mixed flock of herring gulls, rooks, jackdaws, woodpigeons, collared doves and carrion crows circling and criss-crossing the valley. I hesitate at the path in front of the Apiary (after getting stung in my right ear at exactly the same time yesterday morning), but I am

Lawyer's wig   *Fly agaric*

Caesar's amanita

Gray cap

soon safely past the beehives. Even before entering the Jungle the strong, musty, autumnal smell of decaying leaves is heavy on the breeze. Within the woodland itself there is an all-pervading odour of fungi, thousands of which are now pouring out their spores by the million to be borne away upon the air currents. There are fewer small birds to be heard or seen this morning and my attention is drawn towards the four pools. Each has its own quite specific character because of their different sizes and depths and the variety of trees, shrubs and plants that enclose them. Top Lake is crystal clear today with just a few leaves floating on its surface. The raft of whirligig beetles is now several thousand strong, stretching in a band across the whole breadth of the pond. Water-boatmen and pond-skaters are very much fewer in number than earlier in the season when the entire pool was alive with them.

22 October

A thin overcast masks the sun today, but it is mild and dry with just a gentle breeze from the south-west. My walk down to the Weather Station is pure pleasure; only the distant sound of a tractor ploughing or harrowing drifts up from the neighbouring valley. As I approach the East Lawn a flock of some forty or fifty redwings passes silently overhead, quickly followed by several smaller groups. These Scandinavian thrushes will disperse throughout the countryside to overwinter here and they will shortly be joined by their larger relatives, the fieldfares, also from Northern Europe. The sycamores and beeches are really showing their autumnal colour now and the seasonal leaf-drop has begun in earnest. All along the Woodland Walk the path is strewn with leaves, beechmast and the empty shells of sweet chestnuts. No doubt the nuts were removed by grey squirrels shortly after dawn. The black and glutinous remains of rotting honey fungus smother the logs by the path and, in the midst of all this decay, a large patch of wild periwinkle displays a dozen or more violet flowers among its glossy, dark-green leaves.

29 October

Generally overcast this morning, with just a few breaks in the low cloud cover giving promise of improving weather later today. The resident flock of greenfinches is feeding upon the chamomile in the new orchard and as I approach they take flight and rise, twittering, into the large sycamore beside the path. Red admiral and peacock butterflies are still on the wing in good numbers – the weather has been mild enough to enable them to remain active – and several are seen flitting among the white chamomile flowers. As is so often the case, I am spotted by the jays long before reaching the East Lawn and several start up with their rasping warning calls. The magpies are quick to join in and soon the calls of both are echoing throughout the Jungle

Honey fungus   *Penny bun*

and Old Wood. While I am taking the weather readings a kestrel hovers over the East Lawn, but, apparently finding nothing to stoop upon, it swiftly flies out over the Jungle treetops to try its luck somewhere else. The Jungle is, as always, full of bird activity, with grey wagtails on Top Lake and goldcrests in small family groups throughout the woodland. While I am leaning on the rail beside the second pond a grey squirrel approaches to within four yards of me, flicking its tail. After unsuccessfully trying to stare me out it leaps down into the undergrowth and begins to search for acorns. The pool is crystal clear today and the carp are easily spotted as they cruise slowly through the still water. The jays are waiting for me in the trees at the head of the Jungle and once again the woods are full of their calls. On my way up past the Big House I am surprised to see a dozen or so rooks gathering twigs from the tops of the tallest trees

along the Georgian Ride. As it is usually January before they begin nest repairs in earnest, I suspect that the continuing mild weather has triggered off this activity throughout the whole rookery.

5 November

Strong winds and low, scudding clouds herald a blustery autumnal morning with the air full of falling leaves. In the Jungle the topmost branches of the tallest trees are bare and shafts of yellow sunlight can now penetrate down to the woodland floor. On the second pond the pair of mallard are once again dabbling, heads down, tails up, as they feed on the submerged pond weed. All around them the water's surface is peppered with floating, multi-coloured leaves of beech, oak and sycamore, spinning and scudding as gusts of wind catch them. The grey wagtail continues to feed along the margins of Top Lake and, as I pause to watch, thrushes, blackbirds and chaffinches arrive, one after the other, to bathe in the shallows amid much splashing and flapping. A few yards into the Woodland Walk a nuthatch flies across my path to land on the moss-covered trunk of a large beech tree and quickly runs around to hide from my view

Beech leaves and mast   *Oak leaf and acorn*

on the blind side. At intervals along the path several grey squirrels are spotted, each one busily hunting in the leaf litter for acorns and sweet chestnuts. They are now so used to my morning appearances that they no longer bother to scurry away, but continue their hunting and burying activities even as I pass.

12 November

Heavy overnight rain and still exceptionally mild for mid-November. Although it is no longer raining, everything in the Jungle is dripping wet, and with not a breath of wind to stir the trees birdsong appears unusually loud. Among the lower shrubbery the resident robins, wrens and chaffinches

Great tit   *Polypody fern*

are all competing for attention, while overhead the jackdaws clack to one another in the treetops. The field above the Jungle has now been ploughed and pheasants, rooks, jackdaws, carrion crows, herring gulls and small mixed flocks of finches are patrolling the furrows, searching for food in the freshly disturbed soil. Along the Woodland Walk two grey squirrels are squabbling noisily, chasing each other at breakneck speed through the canopy branches, their swearing calls sounding far too loud for such small animals. By the gate that leads to the driveway of the Big House a large puddle remains after last night's rain and a song thrush almost submerges herself as she bathes in the temporary pool.

19 November

A clear, frosty day with ice on all the puddles along the path leading down to the Weather Station. Just beyond the Stewardry a buzzard launches itself from its perch on a fence post and, climbing swiftly, soars out over Old Wood. A little further on, a pair of pied wagtails are feeding on the recently harrowed soil alongside the Weather Station compound. Typical of their kind, they show little fear of my presence. Minus 7.1 degrees Celsius is recorded on the ground thermometer but at head height it is just one degree below freezing. Within the Jungle all the greenery carries a rime of frost crystals, making the scarlet berries of the holly

Pied wagtail and grey wagtail

all the
more evident.
Further down the
boardwalk, beyond the third
pond, the coral-coloured berries of
spindle are also highlighted by the
uniform white of the surrounding
vegetation. Higher up the valley where
the sun has already thawed the frost,
everything is dripping wet and beginning
to steam as the temperature slowly rises.

26 November

After overnight rain it is still grey but now dry and very
mild with just a gentle southerly breeze. My walk down to
the Weather Station is greeted with the usual twittering of
chaffinches and greenfinches as they move ahead of me
through the alders by the apple orchard. A little lower

Ivy

Marsh tits

down, the lovely song of a single blackbird is drifting up from the hedgerow on the far side of the field near the old kennels. Entering the Jungle from the East Lawn I am immediately surrounded by the piping contact calls of several marsh tits. While I stand stock still they move to within a few feet of me and flit from branch to branch in the low-level shrubbery. Climbing up the south side of the Jungle boardwalk I spot a movement high in the tall oak by the second pond and am rewarded with the first sighting this year of a treecreeper. Supporting itself on its stiff tail feathers, it scuttles, mouse-like, vertically up the trunk, pausing every few inches to search for insects in each small fissure in the bark. Its pale chest and brown chequered back give superb camouflage against the mottled bark and make it virtually invisible unless it moves. Leaving the Jungle I pause to see if the pair of stock doves are perched in their customary place in the lime tree, but they are not to be seen today. Just inside the Woodland Walk, by the start of the Georgian Ride, the branches immediately above my head are suddenly full of activity as a mixed flock of long-tailed tits and goldcrests moves noisily from twig to twig.

2 December

Misty, mild and drizzling this morning. Another grey, dripping-wet day with just the hint of a breeze. After recent windy weather virtually all the deciduous trees have been

Treecreepers

Spindle

stripped of their last leaves. The exceptionally mild weather and additional light now reaching the woodland floor will quickly bring the first snowdrops and primroses into bloom. Birdsong in the Jungle is muted but, with all four pools now brimful and overflowing, the sound of tumbling water is heard throughout the valley. On the second pond the occasional visiting pair of mallard have been joined by a second pair. All four birds are in lovely condition and, as I lean on the bridge to watch their feeding antics, they appear totally untroubled by my presence. Top Lake is still and clear and the whirligig beetles – not so many now – continue to circle one another in an endless dance on the glassy surface.

24 December

This Christmas Eve morning has dawned with clear blue skies, bright and calm with curls of mist drifting through the lower parts of the estate. My entry into the gardens is greeted by the powerful song of mistle thrushes emanating from the topmost branches of the beech and oak trees in the Northern Gardens. Small, mixed flocks of greenfinches and chaffinches precede me down the path to the Weather Station and the usual rasping call of the jay announces that I've been spotted on the East Lawn. As I move deeper into Old Wood the sound of water becomes louder and it is evident that the heavy rain of the past week has swollen the many streams and springs that come together in the valley. During the last few days, work has begun to clear the dense, self-sown sycamore trees throughout Old Wood and, for the first time in many years, shafts of sunlight can now penetrate to the woodland floor. Where only undergrowth existed, there will shortly be a series of lakes surrounded by magnificent mature oaks, beeches, sweet chestnuts and stately conifers. The re-creation of large areas of water and the opening up of glades within the woodland will encourage the return of many species of wild flowers, birds, animals and insects. The future for this area looks very exciting.

31 December

After several days of bitterly cold easterly gales the last day of 1995 dawns overcast and misty, but calm and very mild. My walk down past the Stewardry is greeted by the usual clamouring calls of jays, magpies, jackdaws and carrion crows and, on such a still day, other sounds from further down the valley: the bark of a farm dog and the persistent crowing of a bantam cock. A mixed flock of redwings and fieldfares rises from the East Lawn and another, of assorted finches, scatters into the Jungle trees as I approach. The mallard are once again busily feeding on the second pond, and I pause on the bridge to watch them diving in unison to collect submerged pond weed. They are clearly visible below the surface as they frantically paddle their webbed feet to force their buoyant bodies along the bed of the pool. As I make my way up the hill towards the Woodland Walk I am preceded by five or six long-tailed tits, chattering to

Redwings

Holly   Fieldfare

each other as they flit from tree to tree along the newly planted section of shelter belt. While watching their antics I am also delighted to see that the catkins on the alders along the field boundary are already well developed – surely a sign that spring can only be just a few mild days away.

Alder catkins

Common frog

Postscript

How wild the future?

The Heligan story is a truly fascinating one, needing no embroidery to capture the imagination. Centuries of genteel living were followed by decade upon decade of neglect and decline until, on 16 February 1990, the slow pendulum of time and fortune finally changed its rhythm and a new era of hope dawned over Heligan's sorry acres.

I have watched in awe as gardens and pleasure grounds have emerged from a wilderness of undergrowth. I have often thought that there must have been one specific moment when Heligan's future was sealed; one event that marked the end of the good times and set those decades of neglect and decline in motion. Whenever that moment was, Mother Nature marked it well. She was to waste no time in reclaiming what had once been hers.

Over the past few years, my daily hike down to the Heligan Weather Station at dawn has offered me the ideal opportunity to observe the resident wildlife and to note the fascinating day-to-day changes that occur as season follows season. I admit that there have been mornings when, freezing cold, soaked to the skin and facing a force nine gale, I have cursed myself for ever letting Tim Smit volunteer me as resident weather observer. Heligan gets an average of forty-four inches of rain each year, most of which falls on me personally during my early morning walk to take daily readings!

Since 1991, throughout the reclamation of the previously landscaped areas, and especially within the Jungle and the Lost Valley, it has been a priority to protect the flora and fauna which, over time, had become firmly established in these places. The recovery of miles of rides and the re-excavation of the many lakes and ponds called for the removal of mountains of silt, soil and debris. Wherever work was progressing, huge numbers of wild plants had to be carefully uplifted and replanted within the immediate area. Restoration on this scale could not proceed, or be accomplished, without creating at least some superficial environmental damage, and I watched and worried as, where dense undergrowth had thrived, vast open and bare areas began to appear.

Discussions as to how the Lost Valley could be reclaimed, without creating total devastation and lasting harm to the environment, were long and detailed. The huge number of self-sown trees (growing where once there had been open water) would have to be felled, then hauled out of the valley for processing into planking. This task would be achieved with the help of heavy horses, rather than with heavy machinery. The use of these gentle but immensely strong animals would minimize the damage to the soil structure and leave the flora intact. Trimmings from the felled timber would be converted (on site) into charcoal which would be sold in the Heligan shop. Just one large, tracked earth-moving machine was to be allowed into the Lost Valley. This would be required to shift the huge quantities of silt that were to be redistributed along the valley floor. These silt deposits had built up to become several feet thick, so that there was no longer the slightest hint of where the original water levels had been. The enormous digger would make one journey only into the valley and (to minimize the potential for damage) its movement would be restricted to those areas that would eventually be below the waterline of the re-emerging lakes. In this way, it was hoped that the diverse flora on the steep valley slopes would be protected.

When the work eventually began, in the spring of 1996, I was still harbouring serious doubts as to whether we would inflict irreversible harm to this wild and overgrown area. However, I need not have worried; the speed with which Mother Nature repaired the damage had to be seen to be believed. Within a few short months the newly cleared woodland glades, together with the now brimming lakes and ponds, were attracting back many of the species that had long ago deserted the valley. After planting up with oxygenating water plants and a short settling-in period, the lakes were stocked with sticklebacks, golden rudd and carp. This new food source was soon discovered by a variety of water birds; kingfishers, moorhens, mallard, herons, Canada geese and cormorants all arrived to investigate the potential for new territories. Many invertebrate species also appeared: dragonflies, damselflies and, emerging from the water, myriads of gnats, mosquitoes and other water-loving insects. Butterflies were to be seen in considerable numbers, patrolling the margins of the lakes and flitting from flower to flower along the newly cleared rides; brimstone, holly blue, common blue, small tortoiseshell, speckled wood, painted lady, orange tip, peacock, ringlet, wall brown, meadow brown, small white, green-veined white and gatekeeper all made an appearance during the first season. This increase in the insect population quickly attracted bats, for which the whole valley became a rich hunting ground. A survey carried out in July 1997 revealed six species, all on the wing, during one summer's evening: pipistrelle, Daubenton's, noctule, serotine, greater horseshoe and (possibly) Bechstein's. Where the ground had been unavoidably disturbed, the diversity of nature's dormant seed store revealed itself. Countless seeds and spores germinated, producing a veritable tapestry of wild flowers and ferns, while in the wetland areas yellow flag iris, kingcup, meadowsweet, purple loosestrife, valerian, sedge and rush species soon emerged to clothe the banks of streams, ponds and lakes.

Whereas the reclamation of the Lost Valley called for a total clearance of substantial areas of the valley basin, plus the reconstruction of dams, sluices and leats, we were able to leave much of the surrounding woodland completely undisturbed. Luckily, it is within these areas that the majority of our resident mammals choose to live: badgers, foxes, squirrels, stoats, weasels, bats and the lesser mammals such as voles, shrews and mice. The marshy areas of the valley floor, which are unsuitable for burrows, holts and dens, are shunned by most mammals, who naturally favour the higher, well-drained ground. It would appear that deer species are generally absent, or at best infrequent visitors. Red deer have been sighted within a mile of Heligan and are known to roam the area, but no other deer species has as yet been recorded.

The many acres of mature woodland that enclose and protect the Jungle and Lost Valley areas contain primarily mixed broadleaved trees, many of which are ancient examples of their kind. Here the variety of trees – both native and introduced species – is typical of many long-established estate woodlands. Prior to these introductions (in previous centuries) the predominant species would have been native oak, and this is still the case today. However, these are now interspersed with beech, sweet chestnut, wild cherry, ash, sycamore, rowan, plane, pine, holm oak and, beneath these, an understorey of hazel and holly. Many of these trees are hosts to long-established and dense growths of ivy or honeysuckle, offering additional nesting and roosting sites for birds and bats. Along the margins of the woodland, elder, hawthorn and blackthorn are common and, in the wettest areas, alder and various willow varieties are to be found. In several sites around the estate, young saplings of elm are springing from the surviving root stocks of the many mature elms that succumbed to the Dutch Elm disease epidemic of the seventies. It is hoped that these few survivors will escape the attentions of the elm beetle, the insect responsible for infecting their forebears with a catastrophic fungal disease.

We have resisted the temptation to over-manage these beautiful stands of mature timber, as to do so would be to the detriment of the many woodland bird, bat and insect species that frequent them. Where dead or dying trees and branches pose no threat to visitors, we will leave well alone and let nature take its course. In a few areas where brambles had taken over, de-brambling has opened up the woodland floor, enabling less invasive species to re-establish them-selves; bluebells, wood anemone, wood sorrel, violets, foxglove and numerous ferns have all benefited from this low-level maintenance. Ferns particularly favour the shady, mild and humid conditions to be found here and, wherever you look, many different species are sure to be within your immediate view; hart's tongue, male fern, lady fern, hard fern and bracken grow happily side by side. One member of this prolific family, the common polypody fern, has extended its territory from ground level right up into the canopy of the tallest trees, where it can be seen growing from fissures in the bark and along the upper side of many branches.

The large number of bird species identified during the past few seasons gives evidence of the importance of these mixed woodlands: the wider the variety of trees, shrubs and plants, the greater the diversity of food, nesting and roosting sites available. It follows that such a rich area can support a greater number of bird species and it is therefore not surprising that the list of birds seen here includes some seventy different species (see pages 124–5). Two of our three native woodpeckers, the green and the great spotted, are frequently to be seen or heard and, although it has not yet been recorded, the lesser spotted woodpecker may also be breeding in the vicinity. Nuthatches and treecreepers are often sighted, as are several birds of prey, tawny owl, barn owl, buzzard, sparrowhawk and kestrel among them. A less frequent visitor, usually seen soaring high above Heligan, is the peregrine falcon. This beautiful bird has made something of a comeback in recent years and is now breeding successfully on many cliff sites around Cornwall.

The native flora and fauna that abound within the Heligan estate are indeed rich and diverse, as is the variety of wild habitats that support them. There is still much work to be completed here, so the question arises: what will the future hold for Heligan 'wild'?

Restoration and reclamation of the outer reaches of the estate will continue for many years to come and it is inevitable that, along the way, there will be further temporary upheavals. Our main objectives will remain the same as those formulated at the outset of the project: to cause the minimum disturbance to the existing flora and fauna, to re-establish the many lost habitats and, by doing so, to attract back an ever-increasing number of species.

With each passing season we will be monitoring and recording the gains (and losses) throughout the wild areas of Heligan. This will call for an ongoing programme of control and management for each type of habitat. One of the most difficult problems to be solved is how to balance these objectives with our desire to give the public the maximum possible access. Within the Jungle we have achieved this by requesting visitors to remain strictly on the raised boardwalk. The boardwalk follows a route that enables visitors to view the greater part of this densely planted and beautiful area, without impinging upon the exotic flora that grows right up to the path itself. Before opening the Lost Valley to the public (in March 1997) a similar solution had to be found. If we were to protect the valley from erosion and limit the disturbance to the wildlife, it would be absolutely necessary to control the passage of visitors through it. Choosing the various access and exit routes was not a problem, as the layout of the original path structure (when cleared of dense undergrowth) was found to be ideal, allowing the best possible vistas of woodland, lakes and ponds. To date, visitors to this area have respected our requests that they should not stray from these paths, and as a result the numerous wild flowers that adorn the slopes are thriving and, in many species, multiplying. In the nineteenth century, the rides gave access to both sides of the lakes; however, we decided that public access should, in future, be restricted exclusively to the west banks. This decision will still enable visitors to view the whole valley, while reserving the east side as an undisturbed retreat for wildlife.

The renewed areas of open water in the Lost Valley should favour our native amphibians, enabling them to increase considerably in number. The common frog, common toad and smooth newt are already well established; with a vastly improved wetland habitat, they should now flourish. We will watch their progress with interest. Any increase in the population of frogs is likely to attract a similar increase in the number of grass snakes. As yet, these have been seen very infrequently, although they were probably common once – that is, until the lakes silted up and finally disappeared. We have already initiated a project to encourage these beautiful and harmless snakes to make a comeback. One of their main needs has already been addressed, in the re-creation of the ponds and lakes around which they will hunt their main prey, the common frog. Their second and equally important requirement is easy access to piles of rotting vegetable matter, within which they can deposit their soft, leathery-skinned eggs. It is the heat produced within these piles of fermenting vegetation that enables the young grass snakes to develop. Several compost heaps have been strategically placed around the wooded areas and along the boundaries of fields. We will now have to be patient, letting a few seasons pass, before we learn whether the few remaining grass snakes are prepared to take up the offer to repopulate the area.

Our other common native snake, the adder, has also been sighted on several occasions and may be present in slightly greater numbers than the grass snake. Some readers will be delighted to know that there will be no project to increase the number of adders, not because they pack a poisonous (if rarely used) bite but because their habitat requirements are somewhat different to those of the grass snake. Heligan lies in close proximity to the preferred home of the adder – dry, rocky, heathland areas. These conditions are to be found in many places around the Cornish coastline. Here, adders are frequently to be seen, basking in full sunshine, usually on flat rocks or in bare patches among heathland plants. The few adders spotted within the Heligan estate are probably strays that have wandered into a less than ideal habitat. Two other native reptiles, the common lizard and slow worm (a legless lizard), are to be found, living in small colonies around the estate. These shy creatures favour the many miles of 'Cornish hedges' which form the boundaries of fields. These Cornish hedges are actually dry-stone walls, filled (and often covered) with soil, upon which large numbers of wild herbs and flowers thrive. They represent a completely separate and very rich habitat in their own right, offering perfect conditions not just for lizards but bank voles, shrews, mice, many snail species and numerous members of the creepy-crawly fraternity. These hedges also act as vital corridors, along which many species can migrate from one area to another.

Following decades of 'land improvement', wild flower meadows are now a rarity throughout the country. The wide use of artificial fertilizers, pesticides and herbicides has led to the practice of monoculture, where fields are devoid of plants other than those being specifically culti-vated. Any project to restore even small areas of grassland that can compare with those meadows of yesteryear is to be welcomed. Several likely sites have been identified at Heligan where, with a few years of careful management, we hope to see a return of pastures rich in wild flowers, herbs and grass species. It is, of course, not just the wild flowers that have disappeared from virtually all of our meadows, but also the vast number of insect species that were dependent upon them. I harbour a dream: that Heligan's grasslands will soon be as full of flowers, grasshoppers and butterflies as those scented meadows of my childhood memories. As part of this project, a survey is currently under way to identify and count the plant species already present, and to ascertain the number and variety of seeds lying buried and dormant within nature's own seed bank, the soil. This exercise is essential if we are to establish a base from which we can periodically measure future progress.

The conservation of the wild areas of Heligan is considered to be both an important and integral part of the overall restoration project and an essential investment in the future well-being of this fascinating estate. In August 1995 we established the Heligan Gardens Charitable Trust, a non-profitmaking concern, which aims to develop educational and training opportunities for all ages. The wildlife aspect features very heavily in the activities of this trust, enabling it to attract considerable interest and support from local schools, colleges and universities. For most of the twentieth century, each generation in its turn has failed to recognize, or reverse, the steady decline in the quality of our environment, nor has this been linked with the consequent loss of species. It is hoped that some lessons have been learned and that today's youngsters will be wiser than their forebears.

For all those involved with the earlier stages of restoration, the experience of working at Heligan has been immensely exciting and rewarding. Who knows what the future holds for those who, for many years to come, must continue the good work? Much of the outer estate is still lost within densely overgrown woodland and is yet to be thoroughly explored. I suspect that many new discoveries remain to be made and that those who continue to invest their time at Heligan will find it the most rewarding and satisfying period of their lives. It certainly has been for me.

Wood anemone

Bird species sighted at Heligan

Resident throughout the year

Bullfinch
Chaffinch
Goldfinch
Greenfinch
Nuthatch
Green woodpecker
Great spotted
  woodpecker
House sparrow
Tree sparrow
Starling
Rook
Carrion crow
Jackdaw
Jay
Magpie
Black-headed gull
Lesser black-backed
  gull

Herring gull
Oyster catcher
Heron
Pied wagtail
Kingfisher
Moorhen
Robin
Dunnock
Wren
Pheasant
Partridge
Woodpigeon
Collared dove
Stock dove
Yellowhammer
Linnet
Treecreeper
Skylark
Goldcrest

Blackbird
Song thrush
Mistle thrush
Buzzard
Sparrowhawk
Peregrine falcon
Kestrel
Barn owl
Little owl
Tawny owl
Blue tit
Great tit
Marsh tit
Coal tit
Long-tailed tit
Mallard

Spring and summer migrants

Swallow
House martin
Swift
Chiffchaff

Willow warbler
Garden warbler
Blackcap
Cuckoo

Spotted flycatcher
Wheatear
Grey wagtail

Winter migrants

Green plover

Redwing

Fieldfare

Infrequent visitors (passing over or through)

Canada goose
Hawfinch
Redstart

Hobby
Brambling
Raven

Cormorant
(Wader species –
various)

Butterflies at Heligan

The following butterfly species have been sighted within the boundaries of the Heligan estate. Many of those listed are either locally common or can at least be found in small numbers each season. Others, including the small pearl-bordered fritillary and the clouded yellow are infrequent visitors. The former of these two butterflies breeds in small, very localized colonies around Cornwall, while the latter is a strong-flying migrant from mainland Europe, arriving in limited numbers most years and, just occasionally, in mass migrations. The painted lady is similarly a migrant; however this species usually manages to appear in somewhat larger numbers than the clouded yellow. The hunt is currently on for one butterfly that should be present but has not yet revealed itself. The magnificent purple hairstreak favours broad-leaved woodlands, where it breeds among the topmost branches of mature oak trees. Heligan supplies the perfect habitat for this butterfly; however, as it seldom descends from the canopy of its chosen oak, it is extremely elusive and difficult to spot. I do not doubt that we will shortly add this lovely butterfly to the following list:

Large white
Small white
Green-veined white
Marbled white
Peacock
Painted lady
Red admiral
Brimstone
Orange tip
Small skipper
Large skipper
Common blue

Holly blue
Small copper
Small heath
Speckled wood
Ringlet
Meadow brown
Wall brown
Gatekeeper
Small tortoiseshell
Comma
Clouded yellow
Small pearl-bordered fritillary